A PICTURE IS WORTH...

1000 WORDS...

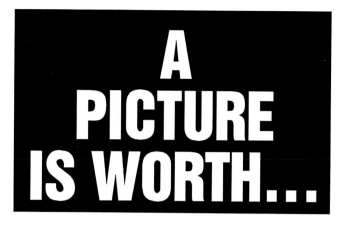

1000 WORDS...

Creative activities for the language classroom

BOOK 1

Photographs selected by
Anthony Mollica

éditions SOLEIL *publishing inc.*

P.O. Box 890 • Lewiston, NY 14092-0890 • Telephone / Fax: (905) 788-2674
P.O. Box 847 • Welland, Ontario L3B 5Y5 • Telephone / Fax: (905) 788-2674

Cover Photo: Anthony Bruculere
Cover Design: Frank Campion, Campion Marketing Ltd.

Printed in Canada/Imprimé au Canada

ISBN 0-921831-08-0

éditions SOLEIL publishing inc.

In Canada:
P. O. Box 847
Welland, Ontario
L3C 4X8

In USA:
P. O. Box 890
Lewiston, NY 14092-0890

Tel./Fax [416] 788-2674

Canadian Cataloguing in Publication Data
Main entry under title:

A picture is worth... 1000 words... Book 1

ISBN 0-921831-08-0

1. Pictures in education. 2 Picture interpretation.
3. Visual learning. 4. Language and Languages -
Study and teaching - Audio-visual aids. 5. Teaching
- Aids and devices. I. Mollica, Anthony (1939-   )

LB1043.67.P53 1992   371.3'352   C92-094004-8

Preface

A *picture is worth...1000 words...* Obviously, not an original title, but effective and appropriate for the purpose of the materials contained in this book. The aim of any language program should be to provide an opportunity to practise and expand basic vocabulary and structures in a fun and enjoyable way. To this end, we have provided a series of photographs to act as visual stimuli suitable to trigger discussion and conversation as well as a *Teacher's Guide* which suggests a variety of oral and written activities in the classroom.

As the late H. H. Stern (1983) so aptly said,

> In the last few years a new view of language acquisition has resulted partly from research on second-language learning and partly from the immersion experience. It underlines the fact that a language cannot be learned by formal practice alone. Much of it is learnt best in the process of doing something else.

In essence, Stern was paraphrasing the old adage:

> Tell me and I forget
> Show me and I know
> Involve me and I learn.

More recently, Pierre Calvé (1985) echoed similar sentiments when he stated that

> It is by communicating that we learn to communicate.

We have opted to use the visual stimulus; for, as we have stated elsewhere (Brown and Mollica, 1989-1990),

> Visuals have been used as an aid to language and the transmission of information since pre-historic times. From the paintings and drawings found on the walls of the cave-dwellers, through Egyptian hieroglyphs and Chinese ideograms to modern visual extravaganzas, man has consistently made visual representation of reality. [...] This is not at all surprising, given the fact that sight is the strongest of the five senses. Most of the information we have about the world derives from the condition of seeing.

It is precisely because the sense of sight is the strongest of all the senses that we have decided to capitalize on this element and to suggest the introduction of images in the language classroom. Moreover, as Morgan and King (1966) have concisely stated,

Most, if not all, people experience images and images often help thinking. Some individuals have such a vivid imagination that they can recall things almost perfectly; this is called eidetic imagery.

The use of visual imagery in learning, as psycholinguists often point out, is crucial to recall mechanisms and the development of eidetic memory, and this, of course, is beneficial to language learning.

Students are frequently reluctant or even unwilling to speak in the language classroom for, quite often, the stimulus is too difficult and requires considerable research and linguistic knowledge.

To assist teachers and to provide students with a useful language tool to achieve the aims described above, we have compiled this book of photographs. A *Teacher's Guide* to accompany this book was prepared by Anthony Mollica, Julie Ashcroft and Anne-Marie Finger. It suggests a series of photo-by-photo activities which, we feel confident, teachers will find extremely useful.

A judicious selection by the teachers will permit these photographs to be used at different and various stages of language instruction provided that the activities chosen are based on the linguistic background knowledge of the student.

We should like to express our gratitude to the photographers and agencies who willingly provided us with a wealth of photographs from which to chose. Without their assistance and their co-operation, this project would not have been possible.

Anthony Mollica

Brown, James W. and Anthony Mollica, eds. 1989-1990. *Essays on Visual Semiotics.* Toronto: University of Victoria Semiotic Circle.

Calvé, Pierre. 1985. «Les programmes de base: des principes à la réalité.» *The Canadian Modern Language Review/La Revue canadienne des langues vivantes,* 42, 2(November 1985): 271-277)

Morgan, Clifford T. and Richard A. King. 1966. *Introduction to Psychology.* 3rd edition. New York: McGraw-Hill.

Stern, H. H. 1983. «And Cinderella may yet go to the ball: A personal view of the past, present and future of core French.» *Dialogue,* 2 (November 1983):1-4.

Acknowledgements

We would like to express our thanks to the following photographers, models, and artists for permission to use the photographs. We have provided names of the person(s) appearing in the photographs when such information was available.

Photo 1: Cec Mitchell, *The Welland Evening Tribune.* Mayor Roland Hardy, students of Eastdale Secondary School, Welland.

Photo 2: Staff, *The Kitchener-Waterloo Record.* Luke Eckstein and Jill Eckstein.

Photo 3: Craig Robertson, *Canada Wide.*

Photo 4: Ken Kerr, *Canada Wide.*

Photo 5: Carl Turton, *The Guardian Express.*

Photo 6: David Woo, *The Dallas Morning News.*

Photo 7: Veronica Henri, *Canada Wide.*

Photo 8: Staff, *The Welland Evening Tribune.* Barry Petrachenko, Joe Pelino.

Photo 9: John Yanyshyn, *The Province.*

Photo 10: Wanda Goodwin, *Canada Wide.*

Photo 11: David Ekren, *David Ekren Photography.*

Photo 12: Dave Hanuschuck, *The Welland Evening Tribune.* Lisa Pinelli.

Photo 13: Cec Mitchell, *The Welland Evening Tribune.*

Photo 14: David Molnar, *David Molnar Photography.*

Photo 15: Dave Hanuschuck, *The Welland Evening Tribune.* Andrew MacDonald.

Photo 16: Grace Beauchamp, *The Welland Evening Tribune.* Jamie Mowat as Oliver Warbruck in Port Colborne's Operatic Society production of *Annie.*

Photo 17: Michel Lipchitz, *AP/Wide World Photos.* Karl Lang.

Photo 18: Roxane Poulin, *The Welland Evening Tribune.* Christian Handman, Mary Beth Ferland.

Photo 19: Staff, *The Welland Evening Tribune.*

Photo 20: David Molnar. *David Molnar Photography.* Ben Bleinman and Aaron Richards.

Photo 21: Staff, *Canada Wide.*

Photo 22: Craig Robertson, *Canada Wide.*

Photo 23: David Molnar, *David Molnar Photography.*

Photo 24: Dave Hanuschuck, *The Welland Evening Tribune.* Barb Schram.

Photo 25: Roger Hallet, *The Globe and Mail.* Corporal Brant Renouf, Staff sergeant Rick Colpitta, Inspector Don Willett.

Photo 26: Staff, *Canada Wide.*

Photo 27: Zoran Milic, *The Toronto Star.* Jason and Jordan Schwartz.

Photo 28: Larry Miller, *Alexandra T. Deys Productions.* Photo courtesy of *Canadian Living Magazine.* Linda Irvine, Art Director. Models Judith John and Jessica John.

Photo 29: Joe Cseh, *Guardian Express.* Aaron Whitaker and Michael Cseh.

Photo 30: Cec Mitchell, *The Welland Evening Tribune.* John VanKooten, Brent VanKooten.

Photo 31: Anthony Bruculere.

Photo 32: Cec Mitchell, *The Welland Evening Tribune.* Kyla Schneider and Patricia Noyes.

Photo 33: Dave Hanuschuck, *The Welland Evening Tribune.* Amanda Gregory, Gillian Grandpré, Brett Grandpré.

Photo 34: Lui Kit Wong. Tammy Gorshe.

Photo 35: Tom Hansen, *CanaPress.*

Photo 36: Dave Hanuschuck, *The Welland Evening Tribune.*

Photo 37: Staff, *The Welland Evening Tribune.* Jessica Motiak, Jennifer Motiak and Shylow Gagnon.

Photo 38: Wanda Goodwin, *Canada Wide.*

Photo 39: Chuck Stoody, *CanaPress.* Customs manager Terry Langley.

Photo 40: Fred Thornhill, *Canada Wide.*

Photo 41: Dave Chan, *The Ottawa Sun.* Patrick Saunders-Hastings and sister Katie.

Photo 42: Ron Welch, *CanaPress.*

Photo 43: Dave Hanuschuck, *The Welland Evening Tribune.* Kelly-Anne Longfellow.

Photo 44: Ted Rhodes, *The Windsor Star.* Kelly Fitzpatrick.

Photo 45: David Molnar, *David Molnar Photography.*

Photo 46: Staff, *Canada Wide.*

Photo 47: David Woo, *The Dallas Morning News.*

Photo 48: Lui Kit Wong. Earl Key.

Photo 49: Ronald Zak. *Associated Press.* Karl Lang.

Photo 50: Peter Battistoni, *The Vancouver Sun.*

Photo 51: David Woo. *The Dallas Morning News.*

Photo 52: David Woo, *The Dallas Morning News.*

Photo 53: Michael Cooper. From the Canadian Opera Company's 1991 production of Alban Berg's *Lulu.* Soprano Rebecca Caine as Lulu and tenor Michael Myers as The Painter.

Photo 54: Peter Battistoni, *The Vancouver Sun.*

Photo 55: John Hryniuk, *The Toronto Star.*

Photo 56: Grace Beauchamp, *The Welland Evening Tribune.* Actress Teresa Kolisnyk in the 1991 Showboat Festival Theatre's production of *Harvey.*

Photo 57: Staff, *The Winnipeg Free Press.* Barnie Ayotte.

Photo 58: Mike Cassese, *Canada Wide.*

Photo 59: Lui Kit Wong.

Photo 60: Kevin Argue, *The Welland Evening Tribune.*

For their research assistance, we would like to express our gratitude to:

Kate Abbott, Graphics Librarian, Pacific Press Limited

Rorry Bradnam, Publisher and General Manager, *The Welland Guardian Express Ltd.*

J. Bradshaw, Photo Sales Department, Toronto Star Syndicate

Bruce Budd, Publisher, *Winnipeg Free Press*

E. Brian Clark, Photo Co-ordinator, *The Kitchener-Waterloo Record*

Wanda Goodwin, Photo Editor, Copyright Sales, *Canada Wide Feature Services Inc.*

Karen Lorenowicz, Press Officer, Canadian Opera Company

James R. Middleton, Managing Editor, *The Welland Evening Tribune*

Laurie J. Taylor, Co-ordinator, Library Services, CanaPress Photo Service

Michael Zeppieri, CanaPress Photo Service.

A picture is worth... 1000 words... Creative activities for the language classroom

*A*s James W. Brown and Anthony Mollica point out in their "Introduction" to *Essays in Applied Visual Semiotics* (1988-89:1),

> Visuals have been used as an aid to language and the transmission of information since pre-historic times. From the paintings and drawings found on the walls of the cave-dwellers, through Egyptian hieroglyphs and Chinese ideograms to modern visual extravaganzas, man has consistently made visual representation of reality. [...] This is not at all surprising, given the fact that sight is the strongest of the five senses. Most of the information we have about the world derives from the condition of seeing.

It is precisely because the sense of sight is the strongest of all senses that we have decided to capitalize on this element and to suggest the introduction of images in the language classroom. Moreover, as Clifford T. Morgan and Richard A. King (1966:197) have concisely stated,

> Most, if not all, people experience images and images often help thinking. Some individuals have such a vivid imagination that they can recall things almost perfectly; this is called eidetic imagery.

The use of visual imagery in learning, as psycholinguists often point out, is crucial to recall mechanisms and the development of eidetic memory, and this, of course, is beneficial to language learning.

Students are frequently reluctant or even unwilling to speak in the language classroom for, quite often, the stimulus is too difficult and requires considerable research and linguistic knowledge. As we have stated elsewhere (Mollica, 1985b),

> Exchanging views on such diverse topics as "abortion", "capital punishment", "the role of women", and the like will not produce in the learner the mechanical ability to apply the target language in a communicatively-appropriate way to the various situations which make up verbal interaction. Moreover, the nature of these topics is such that it requires a sophisticated command

of the structural and lexical modalities of the target language. It comes as no surprise, therefore, to find beginning students unwilling and unable to speak about these topics.

Granted, our ultimate aim should be to prepare students to speak about these and other topics of interest to them. And, in fact, these, and other "hot" topics of current interest, should be introduced and discussed at an advanced stage once the students have mastered an appropriate or comfortable command of the language, have read widely on these subjects and/or have such an intense personal interest that they willingly share it with their peers and perhaps even try to impose their views on them.

The increasing research over the last decade on the development of communicative competence has made it abundantly clear that the spontaneous use of the target language will have to be guided and will have to be taught systematically in ways that grammatical structures are taught. To relegate the development of audio-oral-writing skills to the "Friday afternoon conversation class" has proven continually and consistently to be a fruitless exercise (Mollica, 1985a).

There has, however, been an ever-increasing amount of literature on the development of appropriate pedagogical strategies for the teaching and encouragement of authentic and autonomous communication in a classroom setting.

Our purpose in this *Guide* is, in fact, to describe one of several communication-focused strategies that we have been developing and experimenting with over a number of years. We will refer to them as "visual stimuli" because their psycho-pedagogical focus is the elicitation of target-language words, phrases, sentences and entire discourse units. This discussion summarizes and refines the points made in previous studies (Mollica 1985a, 1985b, 1981, 1979a, 1979b, 1978, 1976).

THE STIMULUS

Psycholinguistically, a stimulus can be defined to be any physiological or sensorial phenomenon to which an organism will respond according to some predictable pattern of behaviour. The "visual" stimulus has been deliberately chosen to elicit either oral or written responses, depending on the language skill teachers will wish to focus on.

It is important to note that some stimuli are better suited for oral interaction, while others are better suited for written ones; there are, obviously, still many others which are equally well suited for both oral and written activities.

The visual stimulus consists of a series of photographs which may be grouped into the following categories:

• humorous
• descriptive
• dramatic
• tragic
• cultural

Each photograph can serve as a stimulus for discussions and compositions at various linguistic levels:

• beginning
• intermediate
• advanced.

This means that if the teacher chooses judiciously a classroom assignment based on the students' linguistic background, the same photo may be used at different levels of language instruction and will be quite appropriate in multi-level classes. The three linguistic levels suggested above coincide with the following suggested hierarchical stages of the photograph:

• Visual Comprehension
• Personal Interpretation
• Creativity.

These three stages may be illustrated using *Photo 1* as an example. At the *visual comprehension* stage, students may be asked questions directly related to what is seen in the photograph. The lexical items to be elicited will be simple and the structures required to "converse" will be quite basic.

1. How many people do you see in the picture?
2. What are they doing?
3. Name some of the items which are being used to plant a tree.
   and so on.

At the *personal interpretation* stage, students may be asked to express their own opinion about the actions/scenes depicted in the photograph.

1. Why, do you think, these are people planting a tree?
2. Who, in your opinion, should be involved in these ceremonies?
   and so on.

At the *creativity* stage, students may be asked questions focusing on their imagination and inventiveness. In some cases, teachers will want to guide the creativity process by suggesting some possible topics for consideration. At this level, some visual stimuli may be well suited to lead to further research.

1. Write a short paragraph giving necessary information relating to the photograph:
   a. identify the man and the young people,
   b. the occasion for planting a tree,
   c. the location where the scene is taking place,
   etc.
2. Using your research skills, find as much information as possible about tree-planting ceremonies.
3. Imagine that you are the anchor person for a local TV station. Give an oral account of what is portrayed by the photograph as it is being flashed on the screen.
4. Imagine that you are the man at the left. Write a brief speech which you would give preceding or following the ceremony.
   etc.

The point to be made here is that a visual stimulus can be utilized to generate spontaneous conversation in the target language without recourse to some previously-prepared dialogue on a specific theme. Since teachers are obviously aware of the linguistic background of their students, they may wish to fuse all three stages and ask questions or suggest assignments which involve visual comprehension, interpretation and creativity.

The activities we suggest below for using photographs are not meant to be exhaustive, but rather are intended to aid the teacher to provide contextualized, meaningful oral exchanges or written assignments in the language classroom. They constitute a type of triggering device which should start conversation on a specific theme in an autonomous way.

GENERAL PEDAGOGICAL APPLICATIONS

The following are some general pedagogical applications which may be used by the teacher whenever s/he feels them appropriate. They are not being presented in a pre-established hierarchical structure, but we are confident that teachers will first emphasize the speaking skill and then reinforce it with writing activities. Talking about the visual stimulus before the written assignment allows students to gather the necessary vocabulary they need as well as to help organize their thoughts in a logical sequence and thus enrich the writing activity.

Vocabulary Brainstorming

Students may be asked to do some brainstorming. For this task, students may be divided into pairs or into a small group and asked to jot down on paper as much vocabulary as possible elicited by the visual representation in the photograph. It is obvious that each student will contribute according to his/her linguistic background and the end-result will be a comprehensive, if not exhaustive, list of varied and interesting lexical items. If the exercise is being done in a language other than English, students should be encouraged to consult a dictionary, a native speaker who may be in the classroom, or even the teacher, in order to provide as many words as possible which will enrich the speaking or writing experience.

Questions/Answers

Students may be asked to speak solely about the photograph. Teachers may

decide to select only those questions based on the photo, the answers to which can be given by looking at the image. Since the teacher is aware of the linguistic background the student has, s/he will be able to choose questions which will elicit the correct response and involve the student at a certain level.

Questions/Answers activities, if logically and sequentially planned, may lead to a short written paragraph.

The Five "W"s

Teachers should constantly remind their students to attempt to answer the questions

- *Who...?*
- *What...?*
- *Where...?*
- *When...?*
- *Why...?*

The answers to these and other similar questions are very suitable at the "visual comprehension" stage and, if asked often, will instill a sense of inquisitiveness in the learners and sharpen their visual acuity.

Word/Line/Paragraph Captions

Students may be asked to write a caption for the photograph. Here the students will examine the photograph and come up with an appropriate caption. This will be an excellent exercise since the students will have to compress in a short phrase or in two or three words the spirit of the scene. For example, the original photograph showing a set of twins in a fountain *(Photo 27)* was labelled "Two hot", focusing on an English pun; the original caption of the three youths sitting on a bench *(Photo 31)* was identified as "A situation well in hand". Students should be encouraged to think of both serious and humorous captions. These can come from everyday language or crystallized language (namely, proverbs, maxims, etc.)

Newspaper articles

Teachers may ask students to write an

article for a local or school newspaper (or for a year book) based on the activities seen in the photograph. To assist each other students may be grouped together and brainstorm the lexical items and ideas or descriptions they would like to see included. Teachers may help by answering vocabulary questions or the students may seek the answers in a dictionary.

Radio/TV announcements

Teachers may ask students to assume the role of a newscaster and to describe verbally the activities portrayed in the photograph. In this case, obviously, the emphasis will be on the speaking.

Before and after sequence

In a discussion on cartoons, Roger Tremblay (1987) pointed out that vignettes are often pictures in a "state of imbalance"; that is, there is something which has taken place before the photo was taken and something which will follow.

Since students are provided with the "middle" photo, they should be encouraged to imagine the events which happened before and after. They will, as a result of this activity, invent or create a story with a beginning, middle and an end.

Kim's Game

This is the popular memory game in which students are shown the photograph for a pre-determined number of seconds and then asked questions on what they saw. For this activity a copy of the photograph should be given to the students who are asked to look at it for a pre-determined number of seconds. They will then be required to turn it over and then the teacher asks a series of questions. This activity works best with photographs showing people demonstrating or protesting, with photos depicting accident scenes or with photographs which are full of details. Depending on the depth and the number of questions the teacher may wish to ask, this game can be played with practically all photos. All questions will focus on visual recall.

Problem-solving

Since photographs are in a "state of imbalance", the teacher may want to elicit from students the problem since the solution has already been shown by the photograph. *Photo 2* is a good example. Here, obviously, the little girl could not reach the fountain and enlisted the help of her sister.

Description of events preceding the scene depicted on the photograph.		Description of events following the scene depicted on the photograph.
"Before"	Photo in the "state of imbalance"	"After"

Cause/Effect

Some photographs will show an effect to a given cause; others may show a cause which may produce varied effects. Students may be asked to identify either one or the other or both. See *Photo 5.*

Editorials

Some photographs lend themselves quite well as a stimulus for Editorials. For example, a photo showing a child drinking from a public fountain *(Photo 4)* may lead to the importance of water in various cultures. North Americans use it to cultivate their lawns, wash their cars, etc. In many parts of the world there is a shortage of water, people drink bottled water, etc.

Public Speaking

The visual stimulus is also suitable for "public speaking" presentations. Students are asked to speak about the photo or use the photo as a point of departure. A discussion of ethics could be done for *Photo 31* ("A situation well in hand").

Writing Poetry

The photograph is also an effective stimulus for poetry writing. Many colleagues are reluctant to introduce or indeed teach poetry in the classroom and yet many students are «closet poets». They tend to be so because poetry is personal and they may be unwilling to reveal their personal feelings. If the stimulus is visual, students will focus on it rather on their personal experiences which they may not want to share and will produce very good results. Why poetry? Poetic writing demands preciseness. The word *precise* embodies the ideas of delineation and limit. Writing poetically helps children develop this language skill. The suggestions we are putting forth for consideration are «recipes» which students can follow with little or no difficulty. To assist them at the early stages of poetry writing, we recommend that they be asked to co-author their poetry by working in pairs or in groups.

The following are some suitable examples but the choices are certainly not exhaustive:

a) *The cinquain*

After learning the present tense and the agreement of adjectives, students may be asked to become «instant» poets by following these rules:

1. On the first line, write down a noun: a person, a place or thing.
2. On the line below that, write two adjectives (or two present participles, or two past participles). Separate the adjectives by a comma.
3. On the third line, write three verbs that tell what the noun on the first line does. Separate the verbs by commas.
4. On the fourth line, write a thought about the noun. A short sentence will be quite acceptable.
5. On the fifth line, repeat the word you wrote on the first line or write down a synonym or some other related word.

b) *The diamante*
Students should be asked to follow these suggestions:

1. On the first line, write down a noun.
2. On the second line, write down two adjectives describing the noun. Separate the adjectives by a comma.
3. On the third line write three participles.
4. On the fourth line, write down four nouns related to the subject. (The second two nouns may have opposite meanings from the subject.)
5. On the fifth line, write three participles indicating change or development of the subject.
6. On the sixth line, write two adjectives carrying on the idea of change or development.
7. On the seventh line, write a noun that is the opposite of the subject.

c) *The Haiku*

The *haiku* is a Japanese unrhymed poem about nature and the seasons of the year. Several questions contained in the *Guide* refer to seasons. It may be appropriate for students to write a haiku poem for those photographs. The haiku has three lines and totals seventeen syllables. Students do not have to follow the syllabic count exactly but they should use a word that hints of the season of the year as they write these nature poems. The simplicity of the form of this type of poetry centers in its syllable count. The Haiku has seventeen syllables divided into lines of five, seven and five syllables. Students should keep in mind that the seventeen syllable count serves as a guide for writing a haiku; it is not a stringent, inflexible rule.

Sequencing

Teachers may wish to leaf through the book and find photos which, if placed one after another, will constitute a sequence. While each photograph may be discussed on its own merit, several photos may be grouped together to form a story. For example,

> Photo 32: Confiscating money...
> Photo 56: Arresting the suspects...
> Photo 6: Spectators' reactions...
> Photo 3: Reporter phoning in the story...
> Photo 4: Reading newspaper story...

Bulletin Board Displays

The photographs are published in such a way so that the first large photo will serve as a basis for individual or group work. The second photo, in reduced size, with a lot of space around it, has been so designed to allow students to write/type their assignment on the page. This can then be posted on the bulletin board for display. Since the photos and the assignments will vary, this activity will provide reading material for the entire class.

CONCLUSION

The visual element, then, is an effective stimulus to trigger conversation in the classroom. It is by no means the only solution but it will certainly contribute to meaningful verbal and written activities. If used at different levels, it will answer the learner's linguistic needs and will provide hours of enjoyment and learning.

References

Brown, James W. and Anthony Mollica. 1988-1989. *Essays on Visual Semiotics*. Toronto: University of Victoria Semiotic Circle.

Mollica, Anthony. 1985a. "Not for Friday Afternoons Only!: The Calendar of Memorable Events as a Stimulus for Communicative Activities", *The Canadian Modern Language Review/La Revue canadienne des langues vivantes*, 42, 2 (November): 487-511.

Mollica, Anthony, 1985b. "Oral Stimuli for the Language Classroom", in Pia Kleber and Marcel Danesi, eds. *Language Teaching Strategies*, Vol. 1. Toronto: The Faculty of Arts and Science, 1985. Pp. 39-53.

Mollica, Anthony. 1981. "Visual Puzzles in the Second-Language Classroom", *The Canadian Modern Language Review/La Revue canadienne des langues vivantes*, 37, 3 (March): 583-628.

Mollica, Anthony. 1979a. *"A Tiger in Your Tank*: Advertisements in the Language Classroom", *The Canadian Modern Language Review/La Revue canadienne des langues vivantes*, 35, 4(May): 697-743.

Mollica, Anthony. 1979b. "Print and Non-Print Materials: Adapting for Classroom Use" in June K. Phillips, ed., *Building on Experience - Building for Success*. ACTFL Foreign Language Education Series, Volume 10. Skokie, IL: National Textbook Company, 1979. Pp. 157-198.

Mollica, Anthony 1978. "The Film Advertisement: A Source for Language Activities", *The Canadian Modern Language Review/La Revue canadienne des langues vivantes*, 34, 2 (January): 221-243.

Mollica, Anthony. 1976. "Cartoons in the Language Classroom", *The Canadian Modern Language Review/La Revue canadienne des langues vivantes*, 32, 4 (March): 424-444.

Morgan, Clifford T. and Richard A King. 1966. *Introduction to Psychology*. 3rd edition. New York: MacGraw-Hill.

Tremblay, Roger. 1980. "La bande dessinée: Une typologie", in *The Canadian Modern Language Review/La Revue canadienne des langues vivantes*, 36, 3 (March): 504-513.

Photo 1 Cec Mitchell, *The Welland Evening Tribune*

Anthony Mollica, *A picture is worth 1,000 words, Book 1.* Copyright © 1992 éditions SOLEIL publishing inc., P. O. Box 847, Welland, Ontario, Canada L3B 5Y5. Reproduction rights are granted for the classes of an individual teacher purchasing these materials. Any further reproduction without the written permission of the publisher is an infringement of the copyright law.   Printed in Canada

éditions SOLEIL publishing inc.
P.O. Box 847   Welland, Ontario L3B 5Y5

éditions SOLEIL publishing inc.
P.O. Box 847   Welland, Ontario L3B 5Y5

Photo 4   Ken Kerr, *Canada Wide*

éditions SOLEIL publishing inc.
P.O. Box 847   Welland, Ontario L3B 5Y5

Photo 6   David Woo, *The Dallas Morning News*

éditions publishing inc.
P.O. Box 847
Welland, Ontario L3B 5Y5

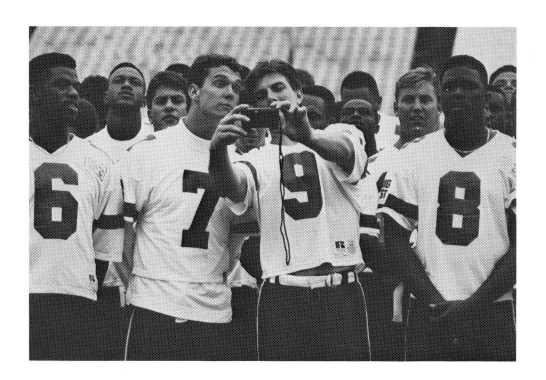

éditions SOLEIL *publishing inc.*

P.O. Box 847   Welland, Ontario L3B 5Y5

Photo 7   Veronica Henri, *Canada Wide*

Photo 8   Staff, *The Welland Evening Tribune*

éditions SOLEIL publishing inc.

P.O. Box 847   Welland, Ontario L3B 5Y5

Photo 11 David Ekren, *David Ekren Photography*

éditions *publishing inc.*
P.O. Box 847
Welland, Ontario L3B 5Y5

éditions SOLEIL *publishing inc.*
P.O. Box 847   Welland, Ontario L3B 5Y5

éditions SOLEIL publishing inc.

P.O. Box 847   Welland, Ontario L3B 5Y5

Anthony Mollica, *A picture is worth... 1000 words... Book 1*. Copyright © 1992 éditions SOLEIL publishing inc., P. O. Box 847, Welland, Ontario, Canada L3B 5Y5. Reproduction rights are granted for the classes of an individual teacher purchasing these materials. Any further reproduction without the written permission of the publisher is an infringement of the copyright law.   Printed in Canada

éditions SOLEIL publishing inc.

P.O. Box 847   Welland, Ontario L3B 5Y5

Photo 14 David Molnar, *David Molnar Photography*

Anthony Mollica, *A picture is worth 1,000 words, Book 1.* Copyright © 1992 éditions SOLEIL publishing inc. P. O. Box 847, Welland, Ontario, Canada L3B 5Y5. Reproduction rights are granted for the classes of an individual teacher purchasing these materials. Any further reproduction without the written permission of the publisher is an infringement of the copyright law. Printed in Canada

éditions SOLEIL publishing inc.

P.O. Box 847   Welland, Ontario L3B 5Y5

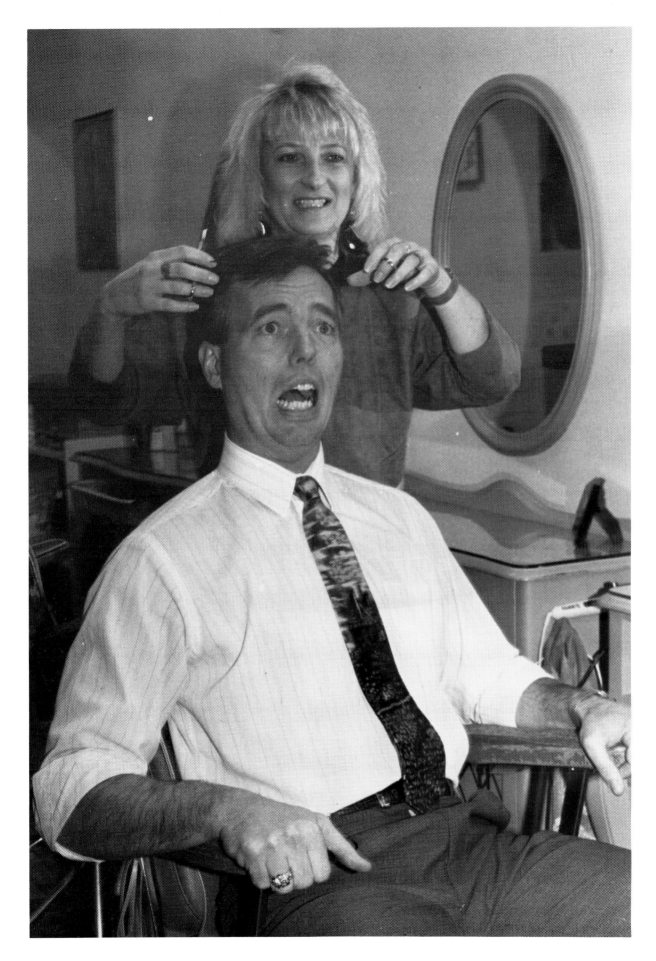

Anthony Mollica, *A picture is worth… 1000 words… Book 1.* Copyright © 1992 éditions SOLEIL publishing inc., P. O. Box 847, Welland, Ontario, Canada L3B 5Y5. Reproduction rights are granted for the classes of an individual teacher purchasing these materials. Any further reproduction without the written permission of the publisher is an infringement of the copyright law. Printed in Canada

éditions [logo] publishing inc.
P.O. Box 847
Welland, Ontario L3B 5Y5

éditions SOLEIL publishing inc.

P.O. Box 847   Welland, Ontario L3B 5Y5

Photo 19   Staff, *The Welland Evening Tribune*

Photo 20 David Molnar, *David Molnar Photography*

Anthony Molica. *A picture is worth... 1000 words... Book 1.* Copyright © 1992 éditions SOLEIL publishing inc. P. O. Box 847. Welland, Ontario, Canada L3B 5Y5. Reproduction rights are granted for the classes of an individual teacher purchasing these materials. Any further reproduction without the written permission of the publisher is an infringement of the copyright law.

Printed in Canada

éditions SOLEIL publishing inc.
P.O. Box 847
Welland, Ontario L3B 5Y5

éditions SOLEIL *publishing inc.*

P.O. Box 847   Welland, Ontario L3B 5Y5

Photo 24   Dave Hanuschuck, *The Welland Evening Tribune*

Anthony Mollica, *A picture is worth... 1000 words... Book 1.* Copyright © 1992 éditions SOLEIL publishing inc., P. O. Box 847, Welland, Ontario, Canada L3B 5Y5. Reproduction rights are granted for the classes of an individual teacher purchasing these materials. Any further reproduction without the written permission of the publisher is an infringement of the copyright law.   Printed in Canada

éditions SOLEIL *publishing inc.*

P.O. Box 847   Welland, Ontario L3B 5Y5

Photo 25 Roger Hallet, *The Globe and Mail*

Anthony Mollica, *A picture is worth... 1000 words... Book 1*. Copyright © 1992 éditions SOLEIL publishing inc., P. O. Box 847, Welland, Ontario, Canada L3B 5Y5. Reproduction rights are granted for the classes of an individual teacher purchasing these materials. Any further reproduction without the written permission of the publisher is an infringement of the copyright law.

Printed in Canada

éditions *soleil* publishing inc.
P.O. Box 847
Welland, Ontario L3B 5Y5

éditions SOLEIL *publishing inc.*

P.O. Box 847   Welland, Ontario L3B 5Y5

P.O. Box 847   Welland, Ontario L3B 5Y5

Photo 27   Zoran Milic, *The Toronto Star*

éditions SOLEIL publishing inc.

P.O. Box 847   Welland, Ontario L3B 5Y5

Photo 29 Joe Cseh, *Guardian Express*

Anthony Mollica, *A picture is worth... 1000 words... Book 1*. Copyright © 1992 éditions SOLEIL publishing inc., P. O. Box 847, Welland, Ontario, Canada L3B 5Y5. Reproduction rights are granted for the classes of an individual teacher purchasing these materials. Any further reproduction without the written permission of the publisher is an infringement of the copyright law.

Photo 30 Cec Mitchell, *The Welland Evening Tribune*

Anthony Mollica, *A picture is worth... 1000 words... Book 1.* Copyright © 1992 éditions SOLEIL publishing inc., P. O. Box 847, Welland, Ontario, Canada L3B 5Y5. Reproduction rights are granted for the classes of an individual teacher purchasing these materials. Any further reproduction without the written permission of the publisher is an infringement of the copyright law. Printed in Canada

P.O. Box 847   Welland, Ontario L3B 5Y5

éditions SOLEIL publishing inc.

P.O. Box 847   Welland, Ontario L3B 5Y5

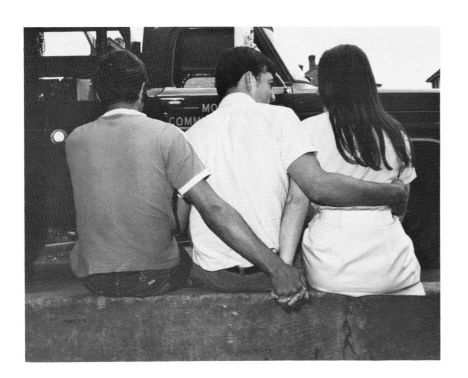

Photo 33   Dave Hanuschuck, *The Welland Evening Tribune*

Anthony Mollica, *A picture is worth 1,000 words, Book 1.* Copyright © 1992 éditions SOLEIL publishing inc. P. O. Box 847, Welland, Ontario, Canada L3B 5Y5. Reproduction rights are granted for the classes of an individual teacher purchasing these materials. Any further reproduction without the written permission of the publisher is an infringement of the copyright law.   Printed in Canada

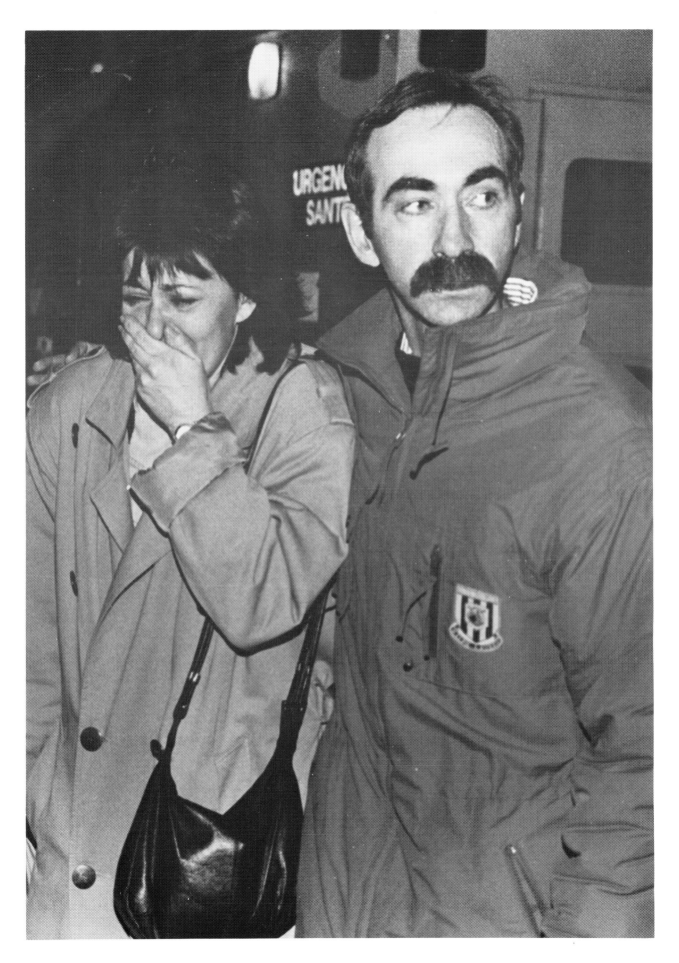

Photo 35   Tom Hansen, *CanaPress*

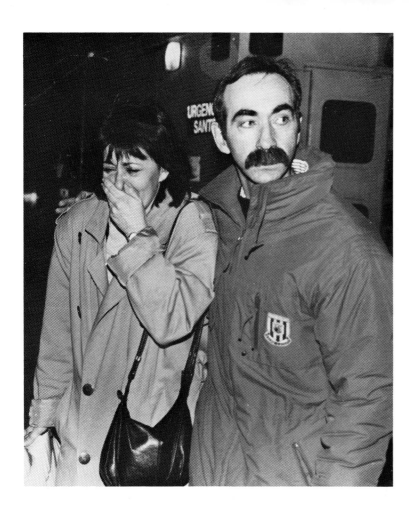

Photo 35 Tom Hansen, *CanaPress*

éditions SOLEIL publishing inc.
P.O. Box 847   Welland, Ontario L3B 5Y5

P.O. Box 847   Welland, Ontario L3B 5Y5

Photo 36   Dave Hanuschuck, *The Welland Evening Tribune*

Anthony Mollica, *A picture is worth... 1000 words... Book 1.* Copyright © 1992 éditions SOLEIL publishing inc., P. O. Box 847, Welland, Ontario, Canada L3B 5Y5. Reproduction rights are granted for the classes of an individual teacher purchasing these materials. Any further reproduction without the written permission of the publisher is an infringement of the copyright law.   Printed in Canada

éditions SOLEIL publishing inc.

P.O. Box 847   Welland, Ontario L3B 5Y5

Photo 37   Staff, *The Welland Evening Tribune*

Anthony Mollica, *A picture is worth... 1000 words... Book 1.* Copyright © 1992 éditions SOLEIL publishing inc., P. O. Box 847, Welland, Ontario, Canada L3B 5Y5. Reproduction rights are granted for the classes of an individual teacher purchasing these materials. Any further reproduction without the written permission of the publisher is an infringement of the copyright law.   Printed in Canada

Photo 37 Staff, *The Welland Evening Tribune*

Anthony Mollica, *A picture is worth... 1000 words... Book 1.* Copyright © 1992 éditions SOLEIL publishing inc., P. O. Box 847, Welland, Ontario, Canada L3B 5Y5. Reproduction rights are granted for the classes of an individual teacher purchasing these materials. Any further reproduction without the written permission of the publisher is an infringement of the copyright law. Printed in Canada

Photo 38 Wanda Goodwin, *Canada Wide*

Anthony Mollica, *A picture is worth... 1000 words... Book 1.* Copyright © 1992 éditions SOLEIL publishing inc., P. O. Box 847, Welland, Ontario, Canada L3B 5Y5. Reproduction rights are granted for the classes of an individual teacher purchasing these materials. Any further reproduction without the written permission of the publisher is an infringement of the copyright law. Printed in Canada

P.O. Box 847   Welland, Ontario L3B 5Y5

éditions SOLEIL publishing inc.
P.O. Box 847   Welland, Ontario L3B 5Y5

éditions SOLEIL publishing inc.

P.O. Box 847   Welland, Ontario L3B 5Y5

éditions SOLEIL publishing inc.
P.O. Box 847   Welland, Ontario L3B 5Y5

éditions SOLEIL publishing inc.

P.O. Box 847   Welland, Ontario L3B 5Y5

éditions SOLEIL publishing inc.
P.O. Box 847   Welland, Ontario L3B 5Y5

Photo 45   David Molnar, *David Molnar Photography*

Anthony Mollica, *A picture is worth... 1000 words... Book 1.* Copyright © 1992 éditions SOLEIL publishing inc., P. O. Box 847, Welland, Ontario, Canada L3B 5Y5. Reproduction rights are granted for the classes of an individual teacher purchasing these materials. Any further reproduction without the written permission of the publisher is an infringement of the copyright law.   Printed in Canada

Photo 46   Staff, *Canada Wide*

Anthony Mollica, *A picture is worth... 1000 words... Book 1*. Copyright © 1992 éditions SOLEIL publishing inc., P. O. Box 847, Welland, Ontario, Canada L3B 5Y5. Reproduction rights are granted for the classes of an individual teacher purchasing these materials. Any further reproduction without the written permission of the publisher is an infringement of the copyright law.   Printed in Canada

éditions SOLEIL publishing inc.

P.O. Box 847   Welland, Ontario L3B 5Y5

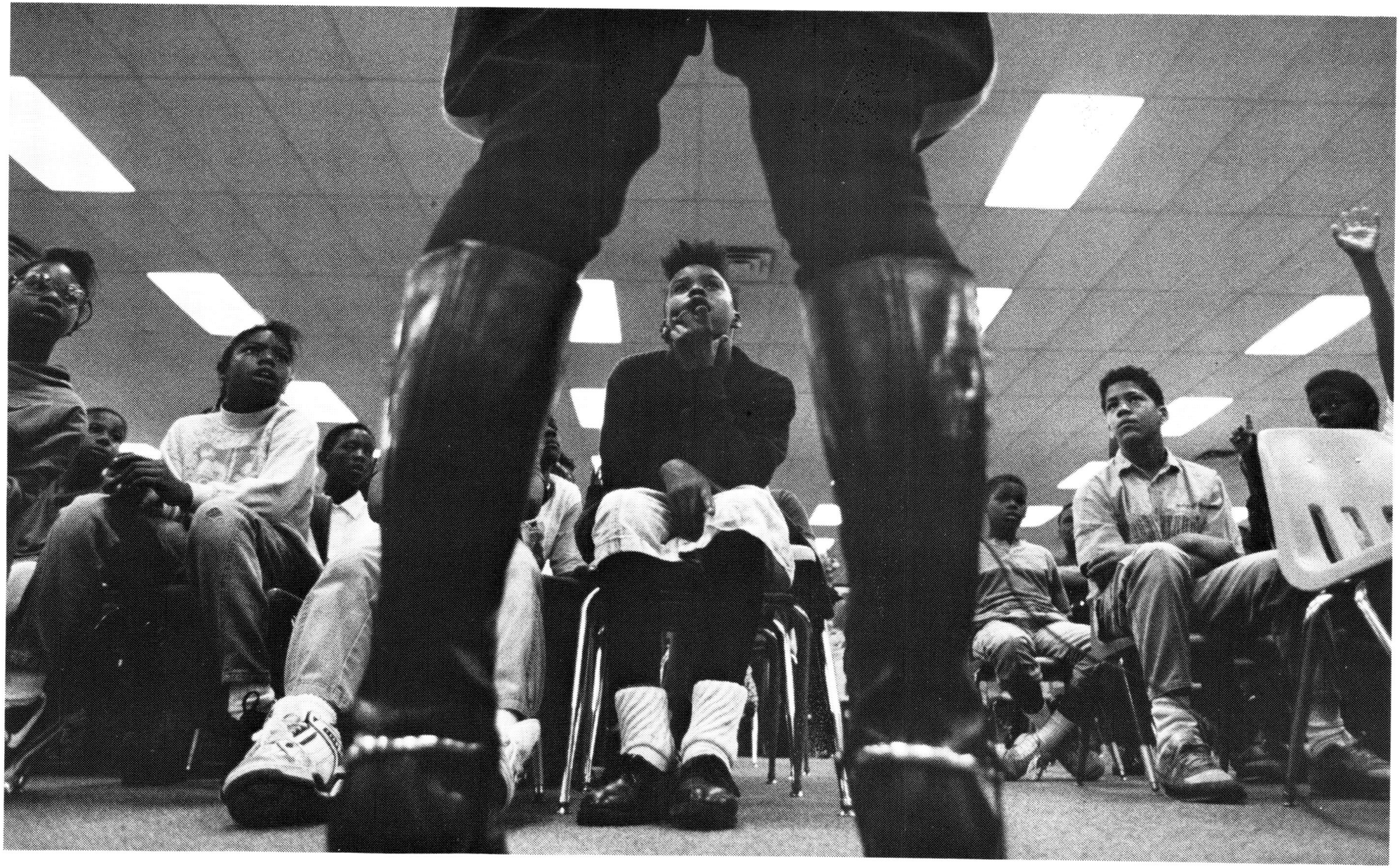

Photo 47   David Woo, *The Dallas Morning News*

éditions **soleil** publishing inc.
P.O. Box 847   Welland, Ontario L3B 5Y5

Printed in Canada

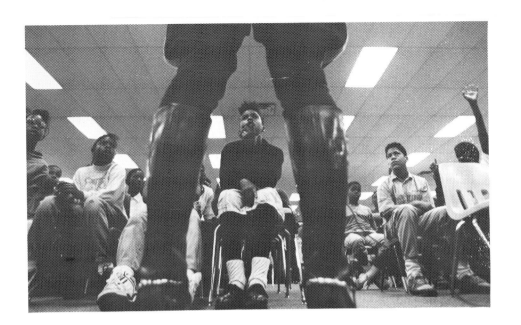

éditions SOLEIL *publishing inc.*
P.O. Box 847   Welland, Ontario L3B 5Y5

éditions **SOLEIL** publishing inc.

P.O. Box 847   Welland, Ontario L3B 5Y5

Photo 48   Lui Kit Wong

éditions SOLEIL publishing inc.

P.O. Box 847   Welland, Ontario L3B 5Y5

Photo 51 David Woo, *The Dallas Morning News*

Anthony Molica, *A picture is worth... 1000 words... Book 1.* Copyright © 1992 éditions SOLEIL publishing inc., P. O. Box 847, Welland, Ontario, Canada L3B 5Y5. Reproduction rights are granted for the classes of an individual teacher purchasing these materials. Any further reproduction without the written permission of the publisher is an infringement of the copyright law.

éditions *publishing inc.*
P.O. Box 847
Welland, Ontario L3B 5Y5

Printed in Canada

éditions SOLEIL publishing inc.

P.O. Box 847   Welland, Ontario L3B 5Y5

Anthony Mollica, *A picture is worth... 1000 words... Book 1*. Copyright © 1992 éditions SOLEIL publishing inc., P. O. Box 847, Welland, Ontario, Canada L3B 5Y5. Reproduction rights are granted for the classes of an individual teacher purchasing these materials. Any further reproduction without the written permission of the publisher is an infringement of the copyright law.

Photo 52   David Woo, *The Dallas Morning News*

éditions SOLEIL publishing inc.
P.O. Box 847
Welland, Ontario L3B 5Y5

Printed in Canada

éditions SOLEIL publishing inc.

P.O. Box 847   Welland, Ontario L3B 5Y5

éditions SOLEIL publishing inc.
P.O. Box 847   Welland, Ontario L3B 5Y5

Photo 53   Michael Cooper

P.O. Box 847   Welland, Ontario L3B 5Y5

Photo 56   Grace Beauchamp, *The Welland Evening Tribune*

Anthony Mollica, *A picture is worth... 1000 words... Book 1.* Copyright © 1992 éditions SOLEIL publishing inc., P. O. Box 847, Welland, Ontario, Canada L3B 5Y5. Reproduction rights are granted for the classes of an individual teacher purchasing these materials. Any further reproduction without the written permission of the publisher is an infringement of the copyright law.   Printed in Canada

Photo 57 Staff, *The Winnipeg Free Press*

Photo 58   Mike Cassese, *Canada Wide*

éditions SOLEIL publishing inc.

P.O. Box 847   Welland, Ontario L3B 5Y5

Photo 59   **Lui Kit Wong**

éditions SOLEIL publishing inc.
P.O. Box 847   Welland, Ontario L3B 5Y5

éditions SOLEIL publishing inc.

P.O. Box 847   Welland, Ontario L3B 5Y5

Photo 60   Kevin Argue, *The Welland Evening Tribune*

Anthony Mollica, *A picture is worth... 1000 words... Book 1.* Copyright © 1992 éditions SOLEIL publishing inc., P. O. Box 847, Welland, Ontario, Canada L3B 5Y5. Reproduction rights are granted for the classes of an individual teacher purchasing these materials. Any further reproduction without the written permission of the publisher is an infringement of the copyright law.   Printed in Canada

éditions SOLEIL publishing inc.
P.O. Box 847   Welland, Ontario L3B 5Y5

Also available...

BOOK 2

Photographs selected by
Anthony Mollica

Detachable Line-Masters for Reproduction*

✓ 60 Photographs by North American photographers
✓ Each photograph may be photocopied for classroom use

✓ Excellent visual stimuli for comprehension and discussion
✓ Suitable for different grade level and multi-level classes

includes

Teacher's Guide
to *A picture is worth... 1000 words...*

by **Anthony Mollica** ° **Julie Ashcroft**
Anne-Marie Finger

The *Guide* provides a series of questions to stimulate the students'
✓ visual comprehension ✓ personal interpretation ✓ creativity

at three linguistic levels
✓ beginning ✓ intermediate ✓ advanced

The *Teacher's Guide* is available in the following languages.
Please specify:

☐ English   ☐ German   ☐ Portuguese
☐ French   ☐ Italian   ☐ Spanish

éditions SOLEIL *publishing inc.*

P.O. Box 890 • Lewiston, NY 14092-0890 • Telephone / Fax: (905) 788-2674
P.O. Box 847 • Welland, Ontario L3B 5Y5 • Telephone / Fax: (905) 788-2674

Kreuzworträtsel für Anfänger

von **Anthony Mollica**

✔ 10 Themen
✔ 80 Rätselseiten
✔ 200 Worte

BK-005

Heraustrennbare Seiten zur Vervielfältigung

Parole crociate per principianti

di **Anthony Mollica**

✔ 10 temi
✔ 80 fogli di attività
✔ 200 parole

BK-003

Pagine staccabili da fotocopiare

The crossword puzzles
✔ focus on a thematic approach
✔ allow students to ex\stablish direct association between word and image.
✔ teach vocabulary without resorting to definitions or descriptions
✔ are excellent for the early stages of language learning
✔ are great for the visual learner

Themes

At School • Sports • Activities • Articles of Clothing • Means of Transportation
At the Farm • At the Zoo • In the Kitchen • Fruit • Vegetables

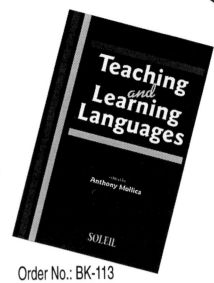

Teaching and Learning Languages

Selected readings from

edited by Anthony Mollica

Order No.: BK-113

Selected from the first five volumes of **Mosaic**, these forty-seven practical and theoretical chapters, written by distinguished North American second-language scholars, are invaluable professional readings for both beginning and seasoned teachers.

The selections in Teaching and Learning Languages

✓ recognize the importance of language teaching and learning

✓ acknowledge the important role of the student and teacher and parent

✓ identify the students' anxiety and offer practical suggestions for studying

✓ discuss classroom environment

✓ provide practical teaching techniques which will assist teachers in their day-to-day teaching activity

✓ highlight the partnership between home and school

✓ identify the fundamentals of second-language teaching

✓ focus on the teaching of a specific point of grammar

✓ propose vocabulary expansion

✓ emphasize the fun element in language teaching

✓ identify methods and approaches to language teaching

✓ assess the neuroscientific interest of second-language educators

✓ suggest caveats with print and non-print materials

✓ evaluate visuals in the classroom

✓ offer suggestions for creative activities

✓ focus on three of the language skills: speaking reading, writing, as well as on culture and body language

✓ discuss the importance of evaluation

✓ and conclude with background information on North American cultural festivities

Contributors:

Janis L. Antonek • W. Jane Bancroft • Jill Bell • Christine Besnard • Paul Cankar • Kenneth Chastain

Caterina Cicogna • Rebecca Constantino • Marcel Danesi • Gina Doggett • Richard Donato

Philip Donley • Charles Elkabas • Hector Hammerly • Cher Evans Harvey • Peter J. Heffernan

Fred Howlett • Stephen Krashen • J. Clarence LeBlanc • Louise Lewin • Cheng Luo • Domenico Maceri

Raffaella Maiguashca • Keith Mason • Anthony Mollica • Frank Nuessel • Tania Onyschuk • Anthony Papalia

Alain Péchon • Edwin G. Ralph • Merle Richards • Perla Riesenbach • Sylvie Rosienski-Pellerin

Roseann Runte • Herbert Schutz • Marjolaine Séguin • Tania Sterling • Karen Tessar • G. Richard Tucker

Natalia Valenzuela • Rebecca M. Valette • Joanne Wilcox

éditions SOLEIL publishing inc.

Order Desk Fax: 1-800-261-0833
Tel./Fax [905] 788-2674
E-mail: soleil@iaw.on.ca